Foreword

CW00336151

Throughout the ages, music has been written to inspire and to tr[...]
heightened experience. Much of this music has since been borrc[...]
other, equally inspiring occasions where people come together. [...]
without singing and every set of supporters will at some time feel [...]
sing-a-long. Songs may be well known, adapted or improvised o[...]
event, it is unlikely to occur without at least some musical accompaniment, proving the
irrepressible power of the singing voice. This collection brings together three such wonderful and
inspiring songs, which have been adopted by impassioned sporting fans but can also be enjoyed
as rousing anthems or encores for any concert programme.

Swing low, sweet chariot started life as a spiritual – it was one of the many religious songs sung by
slaves on the cotton plantations in the Southern states of America over a century ago. There has
been much speculation as to why it has been adopted by England rugby supporters but it seems
that the association is here to stay. This arrangement should be sung calmly but with intensity.

Parry's *Jerusalem* has long been one of the nation's favourite hymns and is a regular feature of any
'Last Night of the Proms' performance (on hearing the orchestrated version by Edward Elgar, King
George V said that he would prefer *Jerusalem* to replace *God Save the King* as the National Anthem).
Since its creation it has been adopted by many as the official or unofficial anthem of their cause
(summer 2005 saw the hymn come to prominence in a new context – this time as accompaniment
to the England cricket team's momentous Ashes victory). Here, the arrangement builds steadily
over two verses to its powerful climax – enjoy the soaring melody.

'You'll Never Walk Alone' originally comes from the Rodgers and Hammerstein musical, *Carousel*.
It was covered in the 1960s by Mersey group Gerry and the Pacemakers. For a Liverpool supporter,
there is little more stirring than hearing fans inspiring their team to greater heights by singing this
song. This arrangement represents a unique blend of Rodgers with J. S. Bach. The initial
Sondheim-esque piano figures gradually start to feel like a Bach Prelude (rather in the manner of
Schubert's *Ave Maria*) and there are other musical quotes included – an *Air on a G string* bass line
and an excerpt from *Jesu, Joy of Man's Desiring*. However, none of this should eclipse the power of
Rodgers' original melody, which should be sung throughout with 'religious fervour' – long legato
lines are the key.

Whatever the histories and contexts of these anthems, it is important to remember that they are
designed to inspire. How ever you choose to perform them, as long as your audience members feel
the hairs stand on the back of their necks your work is done. Good luck!

Patrick Gazard, November 2006

Editorial notes

Choral Basics has been devised to provide arrangements and original pieces specifically for
beginner choirs.

Vocal ranges: the arrangements don't explore the extremes of the voice, but aim to stretch the vocal
range from time to time in the context of a well-placed musical phrase. Small notes indicate
optional doubling within a part.

Breathing: singers should aim to follow the punctuation of the text and breathe accordingly.
However, commas above the stave suggest places to breathe where not provided for in the text.

Piano accompaniments: the simple yet imaginative piano parts have been written to support the
vocal lines. Small notes in the piano part are intended to help support singers while learning the
piece; however, once more confident you may choose to omit the notes, or just to play them very
gently.

Swing low, sweet chariot

Spiritual
arr. Patrick Gazard

5

6

Moving on a little

looked o - ver Jor - dan, and what did I see?____

Com - ing for to car - ry me home,_____
Com - ing for to car - ry me home,_____ A

ah_____ mm_____
band__ of an - gels com - ing af - ter me,____

8

10

Jerusalem

William Blake (1757–1827)

C. H. H. Parry (1848–1918)
arr. Patrick Gazard

And did those feet in an-cient__ time   Walk up-on

Eng-land's moun-tains green?   And was the ho - ly Lamb of__ God   On Eng-land's

12

14

You'll never walk alone

from *Carousel*

Oscar Hammerstein II (1895–1960)

Richard Rodgers (1902–79)
arr. Patrick Gazard

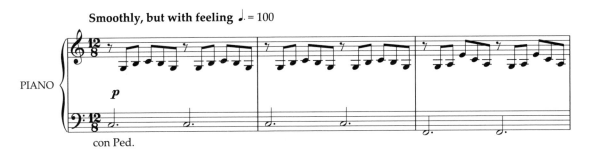

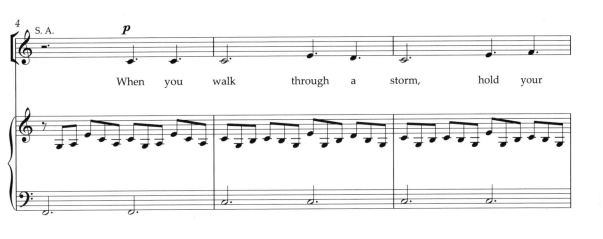

16